Key facts and figures
about the European Union

Contents

Key

B ☐ Belgium

DK ☐ Denmark

D ■ Germany

EL ■ Greece

E ☐ Spain

F ■ France

IRL ■ Ireland

I ☐ Italy

L ☐ Luxembourg

NL ■ Netherlands

A ■ Austria

P ■ Portugal

FIN ☐ Finland

S ☐ Sweden

UK ■ United Kingdom

EU-15 ★ The 15 members of the EU before enlargement in 2004

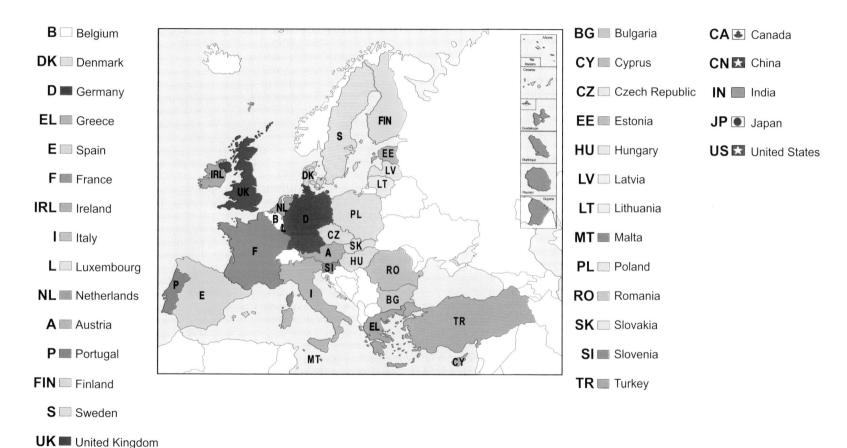

BG ■ Bulgaria

CY ☐ Cyprus

CZ ☐ Czech Republic

EE ■ Estonia

HU ☐ Hungary

LV ☐ Latvia

LT ☐ Lithuania

MT ■ Malta

PL ☐ Poland

RO ■ Romania

SK ☐ Slovakia

SI ■ Slovenia

TR ■ Turkey

CA ⬇ Canada

CN ★ China

IN ■ India

JP ● Japan

US ★ United States

Introduction

The European Union (EU) covers a large part of the continent of Europe, from the Arctic Circle to the Mediterranean and from the Atlantic to the Aegean.

Though richly diverse, the countries that make up the EU (its 'member states') are all committed to the same fundamental values: peace, democracy, the rule of law and respect for human rights. They seek to promote these values, to build and share prosperity and to exert their collective influence by acting together on the world stage.

Over half a century, the Union has raised its citizens' standard of living to unprecedented levels. It has created a frontier-free single market and a single currency, the euro. It is a major economic power and the world leader in development aid. Its membership has grown from six to 15 nations, with 10 more in May 2004. A further two hope to join in 2007. The enlarged EU of 27 countries will have a population of nearly half a billion.

The EU today faces new challenges, not least globalisation. To become more competitive while remaining a fair and caring society, the EU needs to get more people into new and better jobs and to give them new skills.

Using a variety of charts and graphs, this booklet compares the EU as a whole and its member states (present and future) with other major economies. One message emerges clearly from the figures: unity means strength, for old and new members, large and small.

A great deal of further information on the EU and its member states is available on the internet. It can be accessed through the Europa server (**http://europa.eu.int**).

In this booklet, the abbreviations used for the EU member states and candidate countries are those shown on the map on page 3.

The abbreviation 'EU-15' refers to the European Union of 15 member states, i.e. before enlargement in 2004.

For simplicity, some figures have been rounded up. An asterisk next to a figure means it is provisional or an estimate.

Detailed statistics about the European Union are published by Eurostat – the EU's statistical office. See their website (**europa.eu.int/comm/eurostat/**), where more than 1000 tables of statistics can be accessed free of charge.

The European Union – a work in progress

The EU began in the 1950s as the 'European Communities'. There were six member states: Belgium, Germany, France, Italy, Luxembourg and the Netherlands. They were joined by Denmark, Ireland and the United Kingdom in 1973, Greece in 1981, Spain and Portugal in 1986. Reunification of Germany in 1990 brought in the East German *Länder*.

In 1992, a new treaty gave new powers and responsibilities to the Community institutions and introduced new forms of cooperation between the member state governments, thus creating the European Union as such. The EU was enlarged in 1995 to include Austria, Finland and Sweden. The 2004 enlargement brings in Cyprus, the Czech Republic, Estonia, Hungary, Latvia, Lithuania, Malta, Poland, Slovenia and Slovakia. Bulgaria and Romania are expected to join in 2007. Turkey too is a candidate.

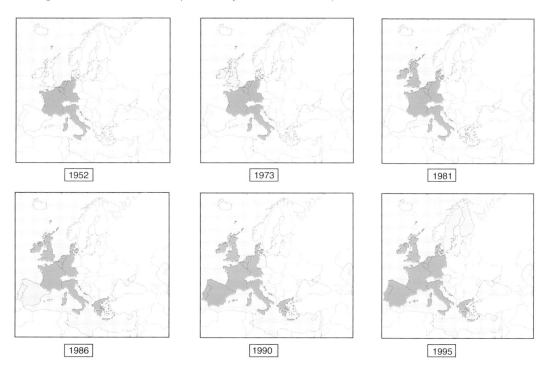

1952   1973   1981

1986   1990   1995

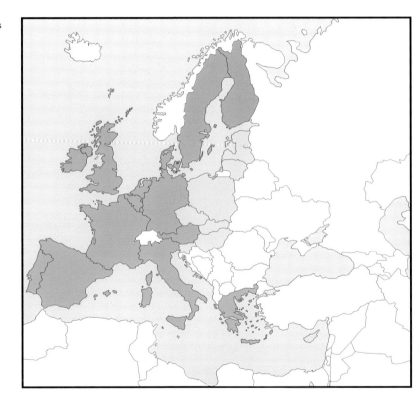

EU-15 member states

New member states

Candidate countries

2004

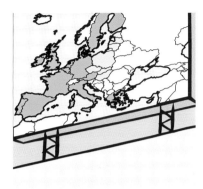

Size and population

The European Union of 15 countries (until May 2004) covers an area roughly one third the size of the United States. Its population is the world's third largest after China and India, and accounts for some 6% of the total world population.

Birth rates in the EU are falling and Europeans are living longer. These trends have important implications for the future.

How big is the EU?

Embracing 15 countries – until May 2004 – the European Union covers an area of more than three million square kilometres. The size of its individual member states varies widely, from France (biggest) to Luxembourg (smallest).

Surface area in 2000, measured in thousands of square kilometres

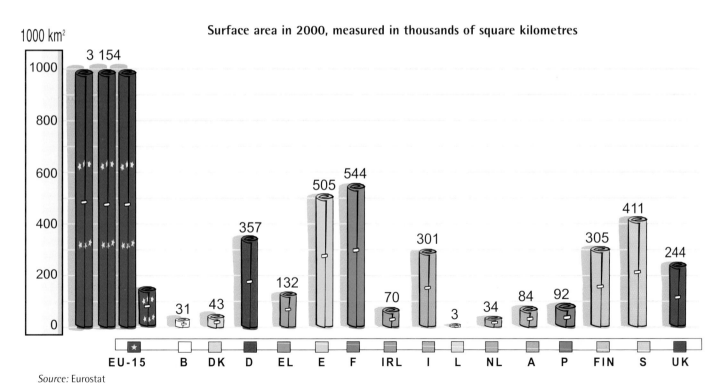

1000 km²

3 154

EU-15	B	DK	D	EL	E	F	IRL	I	L	NL	A	P	FIN	S	UK
3 154	31	43	357	132	505	544	70	301	3	34	84	92	305	411	244

Source: Eurostat

Who lives there?

The EU-15 has nearly 380 million inhabitants – which is roughly 6% of the total world population. Europe has always been home to many different peoples and cultures. In every EU member state, a proportion of the population is made up of people from other countries – usually with close historical ties to the host country. The EU regards this ethnic and cultural diversity as one of its greatest assets, and it defends the values of tolerance, respect and mutual understanding – values that Europe's long history has taught us.

Population on 1 January 2003, measured in millions of people

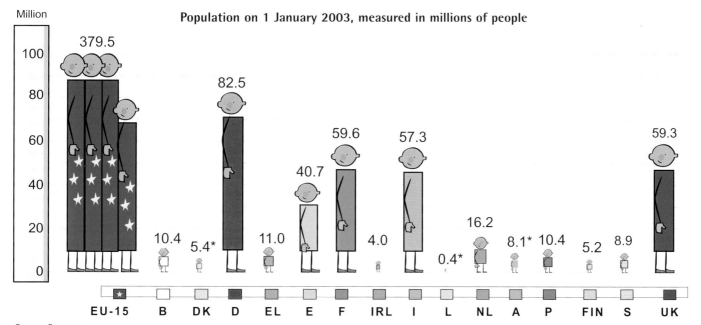

Million

	Value
EU-15	379.5
B	10.4
DK	5.4*
D	82.5
EL	11.0
E	40.7
F	59.6
IRL	4.0
I	57.3
L	0.4*
NL	16.2
A	8.1*
P	10.4
FIN	5.2
S	8.9
UK	59.3

Source: Eurostat

9

The population is not spread evenly across the EU or any individual country. Not surprisingly, mountainous regions are sparsely inhabited while industrial areas are densely populated. Europe's industrial cities originally sprang up where coal and iron ore were readily available. So important were these resources until recent times that the European Coal and Steel Community (1952–2002) was founded on them.

Population density, measured in persons per square kilometre, 1 January 2003

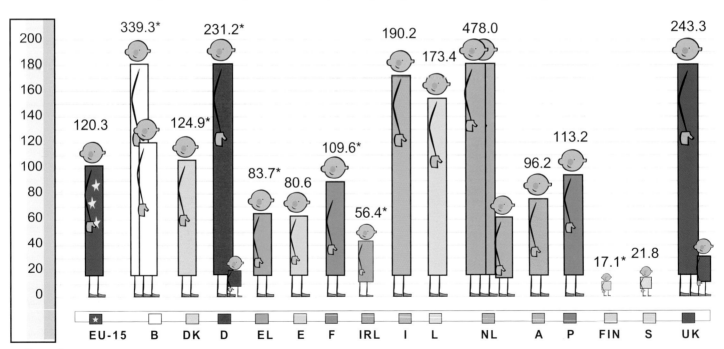

120.3	339.3*	124.9*	231.2*	83.7*	80.6	109.6*	56.4*	190.2	173.4	478.0	96.2	113.2	17.1*	21.8	243.3
EU-15	B	DK	D	EL	E	F	IRL	I	L	NL	A	P	FIN	S	UK

Source: Eurostat

10

How does the EU compare with the rest of the world?

Seen on a map of the world, the EU is not a huge area. However, it has the world's third largest population, after China and India. The United States covers an area nearly three times bigger than the EU, but it has fewer people.

The developed world's share of the total human population is steadily shrinking, while the less developed countries' share is growing. This is a matter for real concern, and one reason why the EU intends to continue its efforts to promote global development. It is already the world's leading supplier of development aid.

Population of the EU–15 and five other countries in 2003, measured in millions of people

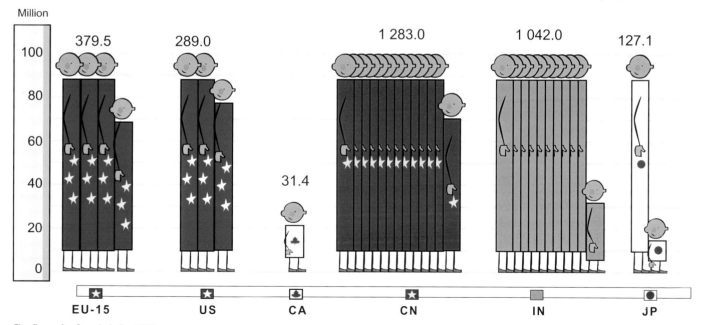

EU-15	US	CA	CN	IN	JP
379.5	289.0	31.4	1 283.0	1 042.0	127.1

The figure for Canada is for 2002.
Source: Eurostat and the World Bank.

The EU is over four times more densely populated than the United States and about 40 times more so than Canada. But it has only about a third the population density of Japan. Population density puts pressure on the environment and natural resources, which is one reason why sustainable development is a top priority for the EU today.

Population density of the EU-15 and five other countries, measured in persons per square kilometre

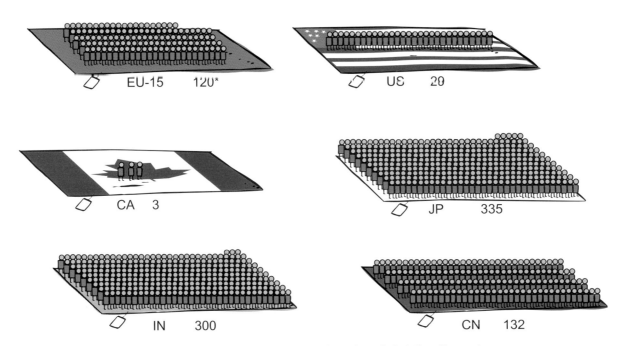

Data for the EU-15 are for 2003. Data for the other countries are for 2001. Data for China do not include Hong Kong and Macao. Data for India include the Indian-held part of Jammu and Kashmir.

Source: Eurostat and the United Nations.

Europeans are getting older

Over the next half century, will the EU population grow or shrink? Predictions vary. According to one scenario (the middle curve below), the population will peak in 2023 and return to its current level by about 2050.

Trends in the EU-15 population, 1960–2000, with projections till 2050

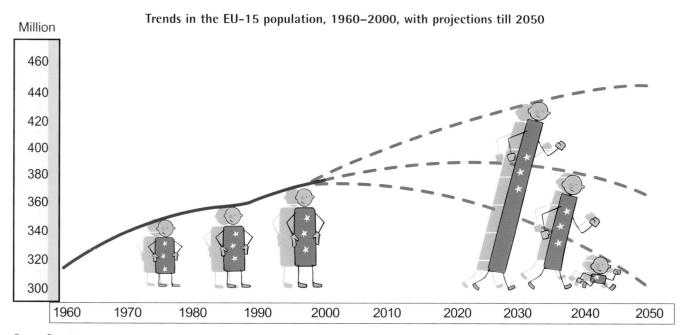

Million

| | 1960 | 1970 | 1980 | 1990 | 2000 | 2010 | 2020 | 2030 | 2040 | 2050 |

Source: Eurostat

Birth rates in Europe have been falling, so there are fewer and fewer young people. Europeans are also living longer. Babies born in 1960 could be expected to survive to the age of about 67 (men) and 73 (women). Babies born in 2000 are expected to live much longer – over the ages of 75 (men) and 81 (women).

Life expectancy at birth, men and women in the EU-15, 1960–2000

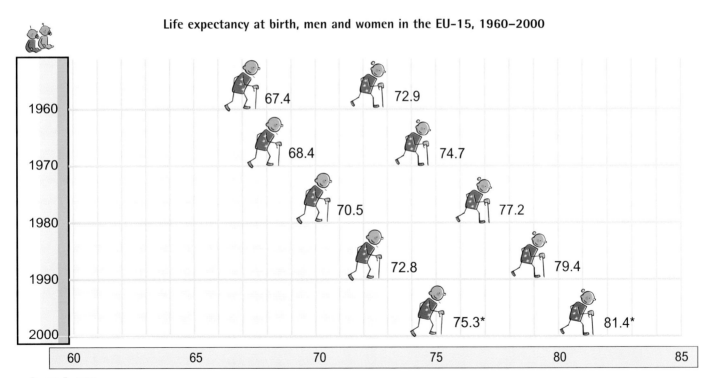

Year	Men	Women
1960	67.4	72.9
1970	68.4	74.7
1980	70.5	77.2
1990	72.8	79.4
2000	75.3*	81.4*

Source: Eurostat

Current trends mean there are fewer and fewer people in work to support more and more pensioners. To maintain the size of its working population, Europe needs a combination of skilled immigration, life-long learning, more women in work and more people working part-time beyond retirement age. More babies would also help!

The following graphs show the numbers of people in different age ranges living in the EU-15, 1980–2000, with projections until 2020. Figures are in millions.

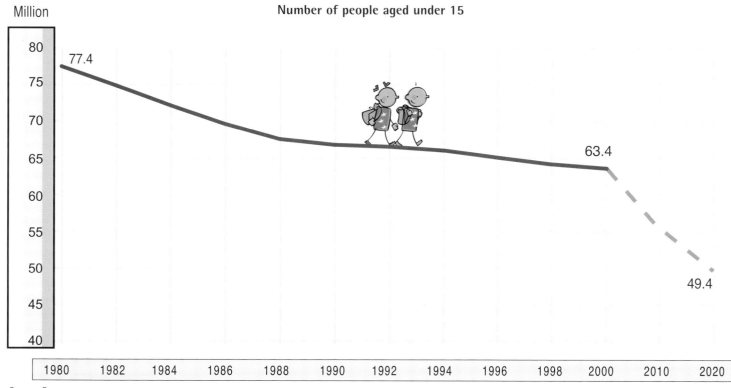

Number of people aged under 15

Million

80
77.4
75
70
65
63.4
60
55
50
49.4
45
40

1980 1982 1984 1986 1988 1990 1992 1994 1996 1998 2000 2010 2020

Source: Eurostat

Number of people aged 15 to 24

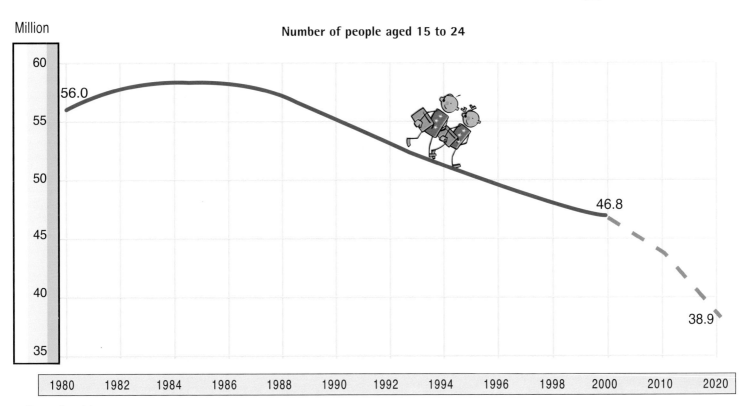

Million

56.0

46.8

38.9

60
55
50
45
40
35

1980 1982 1984 1986 1988 1990 1992 1994 1996 1998 2000 2010 2020

Source: Eurostat

Number of people aged 25 to 49

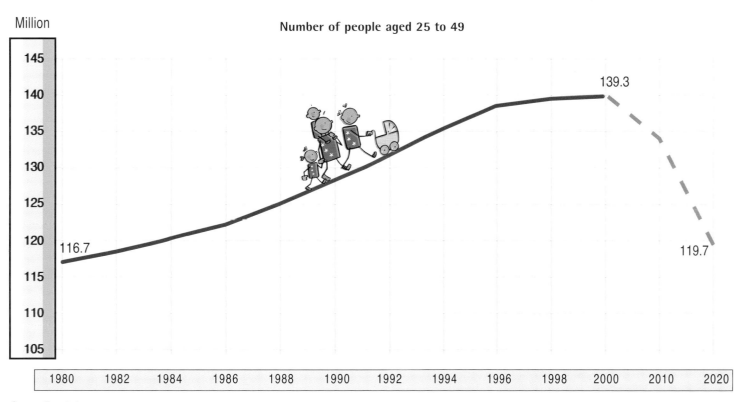

Million

145

140 — 139.3

135

130

125

120

116.7

115

110

105

| 1980 | 1982 | 1984 | 1986 | 1988 | 1990 | 1992 | 1994 | 1996 | 1998 | 2000 | 2010 | 2020 |

119.7

Source: Eurostat

Number of people aged 50 to 64

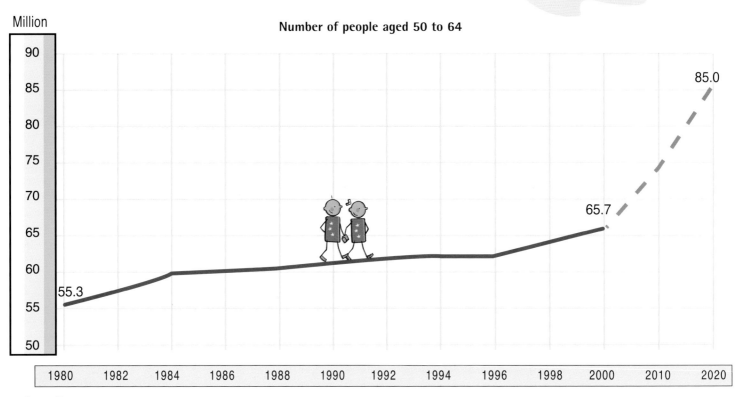

Million

- 55.3
- 65.7
- 85.0

1980 1982 1984 1986 1988 1990 1992 1994 1996 1998 2000 2010 2020

Source: Eurostat

Number of people aged 65 to 79

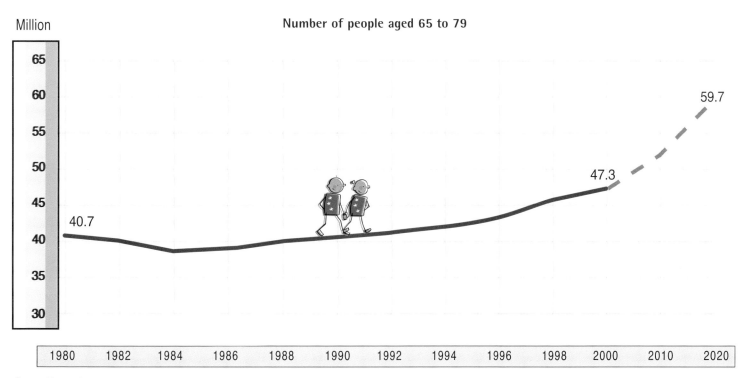

Million

65	
60	59.7
55	
50	
47.3	
45	
40.7	
40	
35	
30	

1980 1982 1984 1986 1988 1990 1992 1994 1996 1998 2000 2010 2020

Source: Eurostat

Number of people aged 80 or over

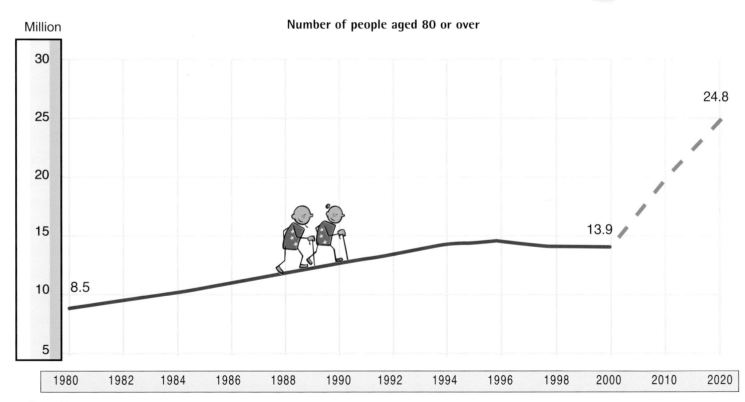

Million

30

25 — 24.8

20

15 — 13.9

10 — 8.5

5

1980 1982 1984 1986 1988 1990 1992 1994 1996 1998 2000 2010 2020

Source: Eurostat

Total population growth is a combination of **natural growth** (i.e. when more people are born than die) and growth due to **net migration.** (Net migration is the balance of immigration and emigration. The balance is positive when more people settle in the EU than leave it).

At the start of the 1960s, natural growth accounted for most of the EU's population increase. But birth rates have been falling in Europe, and net migration now accounts for nearly three quarters of the EU's total population growth. Without immigration, the number of people in Germany, Greece, Italy and Austria would actually be declining.

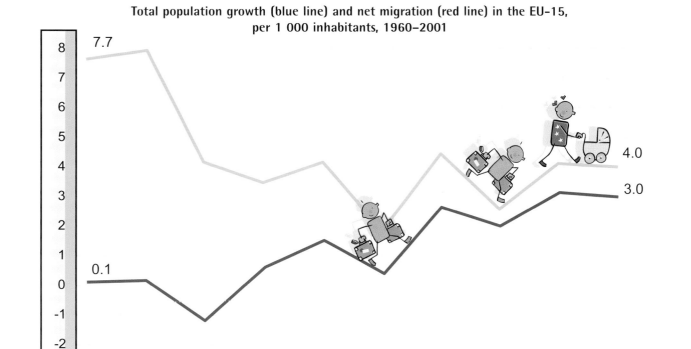

Total population growth (blue line) and net migration (red line) in the EU-15, per 1 000 inhabitants, 1960–2001

Source: Eurostat

Standard of living

How well off are Europeans? What is their standard of living? The answer varies from one country to another. To get a rough idea we can measure the total value of everything a country produces in a given calendar year (its 'gross domestic product': GDP) and then divide that figure by the number of inhabitants.

But prices vary from one country to another, and those price differences must be eliminated before we can compare standards of living. We can do this by measuring the price of a comparable and representative 'basket' of goods and services in each country. This figure is given not in national currency units but in a common artificial currency we call the **'purchasing power standard' (PPS).** Comparing GDP per inhabitant in PPS gives a fair comparison of the standard of living in different countries.

How wealthy are Europeans?

All EU countries have become wealthier over the past decade, and their citizens' standards of living have risen appreciably. Ireland, a country which was relatively poor when it joined the EU, has made particularly striking progress.

European Union funding has helped achieve this, and similar progress is expected for the countries joining the European Union in 2004. As EU citizens become more affluent they become more active consumers, which is good news for European business. However, standards of living vary from one region to another. One purpose of the EU's 'structural funds' is to even out these differences by helping boost the economies of poorer regions.

GDP in PPS per inhabitant, 2001

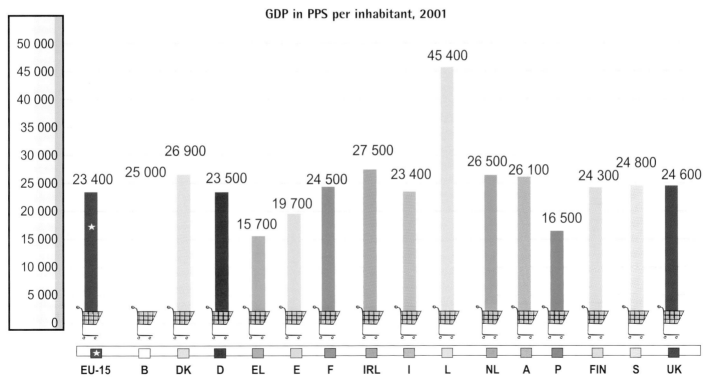

EU-15	B	DK	D	EL	E	F	IRL	I	L	NL	A	P	FIN	S	UK
23 400	25 000	26 900	23 500	15 700	19 700	24 500	27 500	23 400	45 400	26 500	26 100	16 500	24 300	24 800	24 600

Source: Eurostat

23

Little luxuries or essential tools?

In recent years, the EU has seen a rapid increase in the use of mobile phones. In 1990, only about one person in every hundred used one; in 2002, the figure had risen to about 78% and it reached 80% in 2003. The EU-15 is ahead of both the United States and Japan in this respect – partly because European countries lead the field in manufacturing mobile phone technology.

Number of mobile phone subscribers per 100 people, 2002

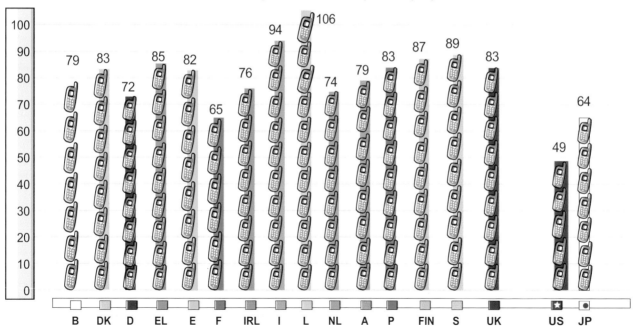

B	DK	D	EL	E	F	IRL	I	L	NL	A	P	FIN	S	UK	US	JP
79	83	72	85	82	65	76	94	106	74	79	83	87	89	83	49	64

Source: Eurostat

The ownership and use of personal computers (PCs) is also increasing in Europe, but Europeans as a whole lag well behind US citizens in owning PCs and using the internet.

Greater use of the internet is a key to modern education and new jobs, so one EU priority is to get its citizens online as fast as possible and to train both school pupils and older workers in computer skills.

Number of personal computers per 100 people, 2001

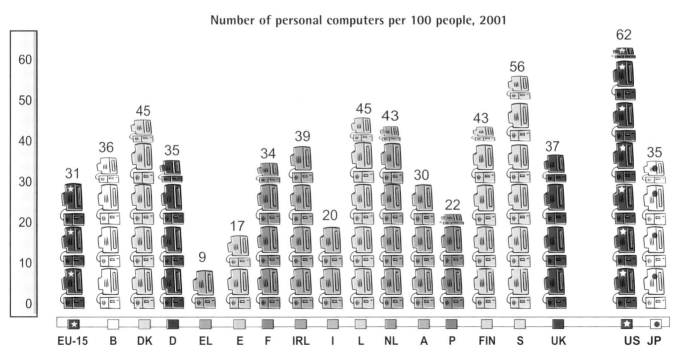

EU-15	B	DK	D	EL	E	F	IRL	I	L	NL	A	P	FIN	S	UK	US	JP
31	36	45	35	9	17	34	39	20	45	43	30	22	43	56	37	62	35

Source: Eurostat

☂ A fair and caring society

The European social model takes different forms in different countries, but all EU countries aim to be fair and caring societies. They redistribute wealth through 'social benefit' payments, designed to narrow the gap between rich and poor and to protect vulnerable members of society such as the sick, the elderly and the unemployed. The overall cost varies from country to country, but it is rising in the EU as a whole, partly because people are living longer.

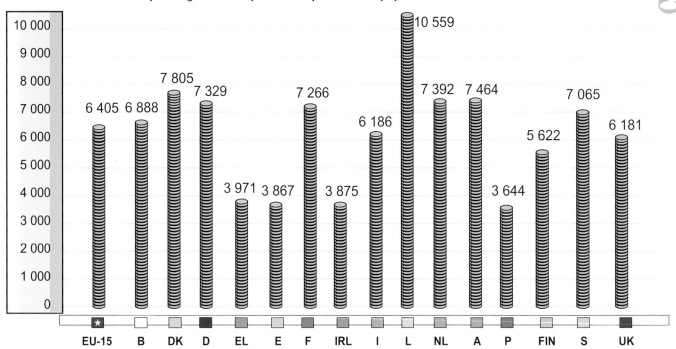

Spending on social protection per head of population, in PPS, 2001

EU-15	B	DK	D	EL	E	F	IRL	I	L	NL	A	P	FIN	S	UK
6 405	6 888	7 805	7 329	3 971	3 867	7 266	3 875	6 186	10 559	7 392	7 464	3 644	5 622	7 065	6 181

Source: Eurostat

As the population ages, a shrinking workforce is having to support an increasing number of senior citizens. To take account of this trend, and to keep welfare costs under control, EU countries are having to redesign their social protection systems. Europe's social model has to be modernised to preserve it for future generations.

Spending on three types of social benefits per head of population in PPS. Figures are for EU–15, 1993–2001

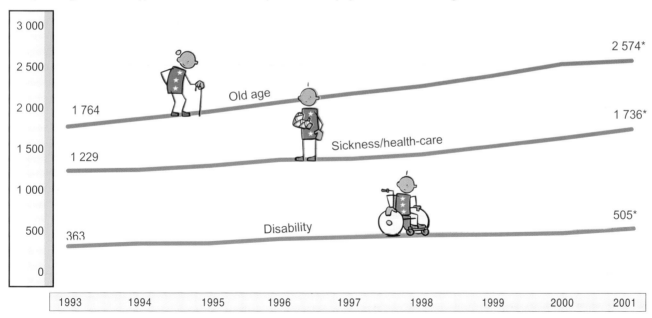

Source: Eurostat

Education and research

It is an EU priority to invest heavily in education and research, in order to boost its competitiveness and give Europeans the skills they need for life in the 21st century.

More Europeans are studying

The number of young people in full-time education, and especially the number of students in higher education, has been growing in the EU as Europeans increasingly realise the value of gaining better qualifications.

Number of full-time and part-time pupils and students, all ages (except pre-primary), in millions, 2000

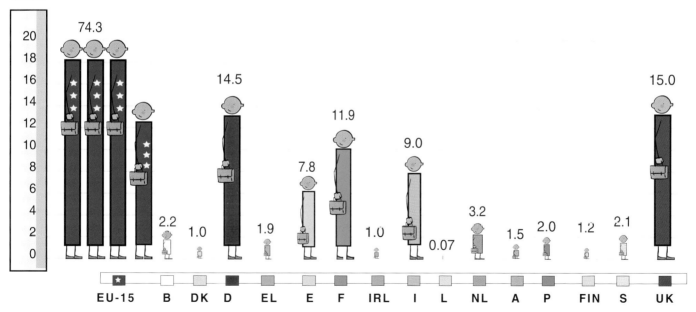

Million

EU-15	B	DK	D	EL	E	F	IRL	I	L	NL	A	P	FIN	S	UK
74.3	2.2	1.0	14.5	1.9	7.8	11.9	1.0	9.0	0.07	3.2	1.5	2.0	1.2	2.1	15.0

Source: Eurostat/Unesco/OECD.

Trend in number of pupils and students (excluding pre-primary), in millions, EU-15, 1993–2000

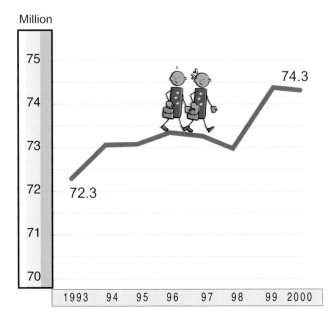

Million

75

74.3

74

73

72

72.3

71

70

1993 94 95 96 97 98 99 2000

Trend in number of students in higher education, in millions, EU-15, 1991–2000

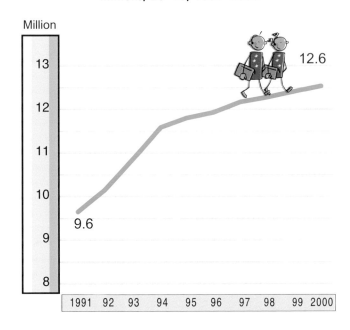

Million

13

12.6

12

11

10

9.6

9

8

1991 92 93 94 95 96 97 98 99 2000

Since 1998/99 the figures for Luxembourg for the first three levels of education include private institutions. Figures for the highest level of education (advanced stage of tertiary education) are missing for Germany.

Source: Eurostat/Unesco/OECD.

Figures for the highest level of education (advanced stage of tertiary education) are missing for Germany.

Source: Eurostat/Unesco/OECD.

Younger Europeans are better qualified

Over the past 30 years, the educational level of the EU population as a whole has been steadily rising. Women, whose attainments were below men's a generation ago, have now caught up or even overtaken men.

Percentage of the EU-15 population, in different age brackets, having completed at least upper secondary education, 2002

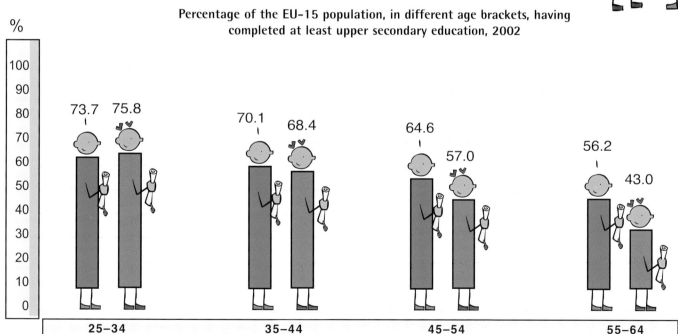

%

- 73.7 75.8 — 25–34
- 70.1 68.4 — 35–44
- 64.6 57.0 — 45–54
- 56.2 43.0 — 55–64

Source: Eurostat

Better education means better job prospects

Generally speaking, and apart from retired people, the older you are the more likely you are to be in work if you live in the European Union. But the less educated you are, the more likely you are to be unemployed, regardless of your age. If you have completed tertiary education (e.g. a university degree course), you are twice or even three times as likely to have a job as someone of your age with only primary or lower secondary schooling.

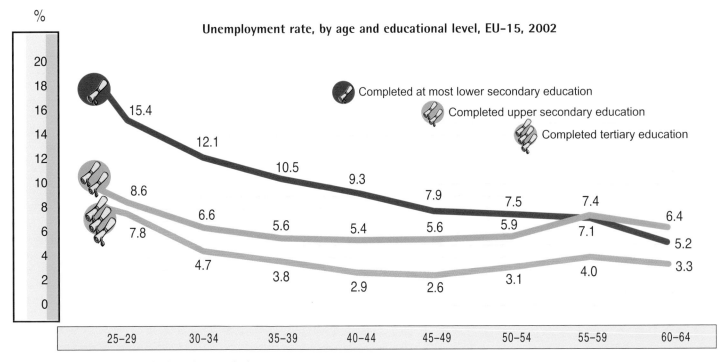

Unemployment rate, by age and educational level, EU–15, 2002

%

- ● Completed at most lower secondary education
- ● Completed upper secondary education
- ● Completed tertiary education

Completed at most lower secondary education: 15.4, 12.1, 10.5, 9.3, 7.9, 7.5, 7.4, 5.2

Completed upper secondary education: 8.6, 6.6, 5.6, 5.4, 5.6, 5.9, 7.1, 6.4

Completed tertiary education: 7.8, 4.7, 3.8, 2.9, 2.6, 3.1, 4.0, 3.3

Age groups: 25–29, 30–34, 35–39, 40–44, 45–49, 50–54, 55–59, 60–64

These figures are indicative only, due to low sample sizes.

Source: Eurostat

Research – key to the future

Overall, EU spending on research and development (R&D) gradually declined in the period 1990–2000, so that Europe ended the decade lagging further and further behind the United States and Japan. But R&D, especially in new technologies, holds the key to future competitiveness and jobs, which is why the EU's new strategy (since 2000) is to invest much more in research. In 2001 EU spending on R&D was back up to 1.98% of GDP.

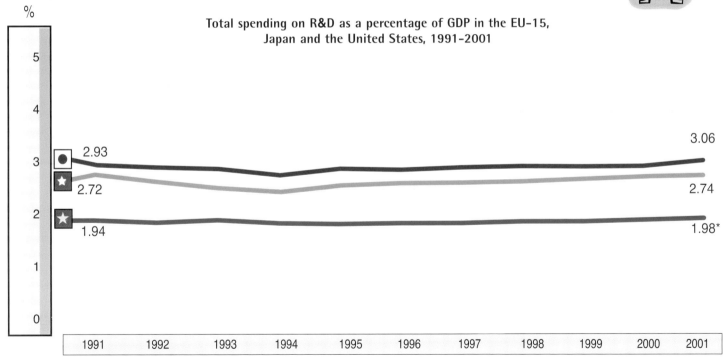

Total spending on R&D as a percentage of GDP in the EU-15, Japan and the United States, 1991-2001

%

2.93	3.06
2.72	2.74
1.94	1.98*

1991 1992 1993 1994 1995 1996 1997 1998 1999 2000 2001

All figures for the EU-15 are estimates, as are the figures for the United States for 2000.
Source: Eurostat and OECD.

The share of GDP that is spent on R&D varies from one EU country to another. Some, such as Finland and Sweden, invest heavily in R&D, partly because they are market leaders in mobile phone technology.

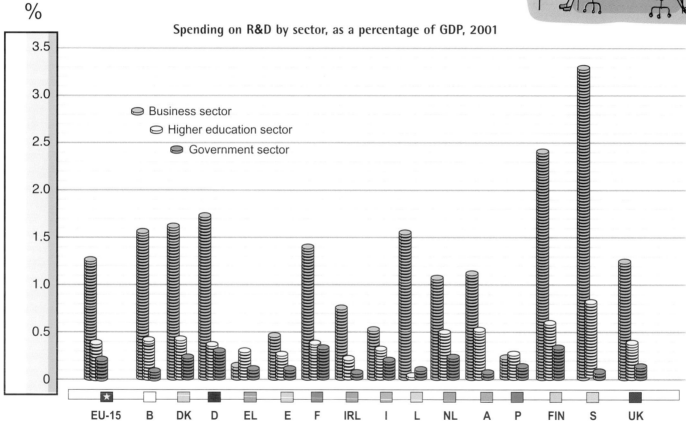

Spending on R&D by sector, as a percentage of GDP, 2001

%

- ⊖ Business sector
- ⊖ Higher education sector
- ⊖ Government sector

EU-15   B   DK   D   EL   E   F   IRL   I   L   NL   A   P   FIN   S   UK

EL: 1999 data; A: 1998 data; P: 1999 data; S: 1999 data

Source: Eurostat

The European Union at work

Employment is a top priority for the EU. Its aim is to become the world's most dynamic and competitive knowledge-based economy by 2010. This means creating more and better jobs for EU citizens and ensuring equal opportunities so everyone who wants to can work. The EU aims to achieve an employment rate of 67% by January 2005 and 70% by 2010.

How many people work in the EU?

In Spring 2002, more than 64% of people of working age had jobs, and there were 1.7 million more jobs than in Spring 2001. However, the employment rate varies from country to country, and often from region to region within each country. It is also different for men and women.

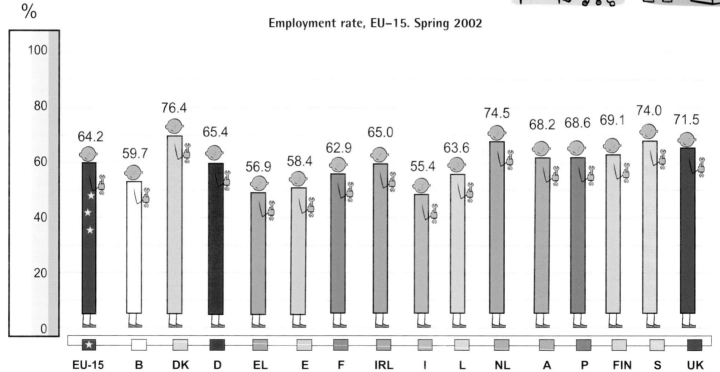

Employment rate, EU–15. Spring 2002

%

EU-15	B	DK	D	EL	E	F	IRL	I	L	NL	A	P	FIN	S	UK
64.2	59.7	76.4	65.4	56.9	58.4	62.9	65.0	55.4	63.6	74.5	68.2	68.6	69.1	74.0	71.5

Source: Eurostat

In June 2003, around 8.1% of the EU's labour force were unemployed, compared to 6.4% in the United States and 5.3% in Japan. Overall, the unemployment rate in the EU fell during the period 1993–2001, and the EU is working hard to resume this downward trend.

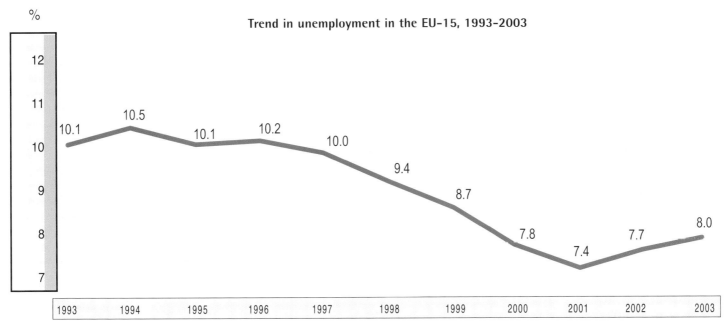

Trend in unemployment in the EU-15, 1993–2003

%

Source: Eurostat

The jobs people do

In the 1950s, over 20% of people in the EU (only six countries at the time) worked in farming and around 40% in industry. By 2001, those figures had dropped to 4 and 29% for the EU-15.

Most of the new jobs created in the EU-15 are in the services sector – which now employs two out of every three workers. Many new jobs involve data processing and the use of information technologies, which hold the key to the EU's future competitiveness.

Number of people working in agriculture (including hunting, forestry and fishing), industry and services, EU-15, 1995 and 2001. Figures are in millions

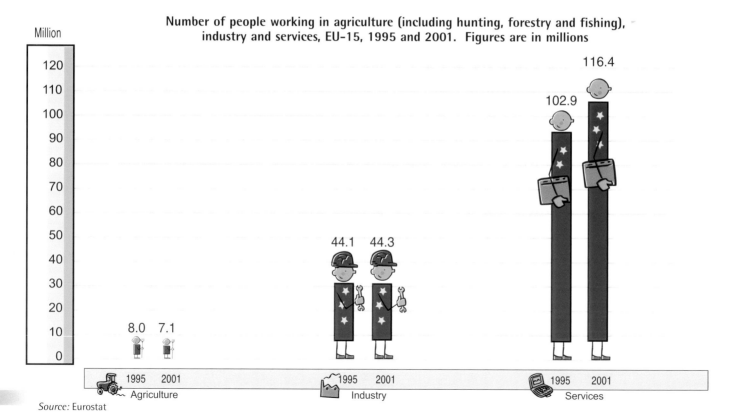

Source: Eurostat

Equal opportunities for all?

In each age bracket, more men than women have jobs and this is generally true of all countries in the EU. This is sometimes due to discrimination in the workplace, sometimes the result of personal choice or cultural traditions.

There is a north-south divide in the proportion of women who work. The lowest percentages are in southern Europe and the highest are in the north. For example, in 2002, just over 42.7% of Greek women of working age were in work, whereas the figure in both Denmark and Sweden was over 70%. Men and women in the EU also have different working patterns, with more women than men working part-time.

Employment rate by age group and gender, second quarter of 2002

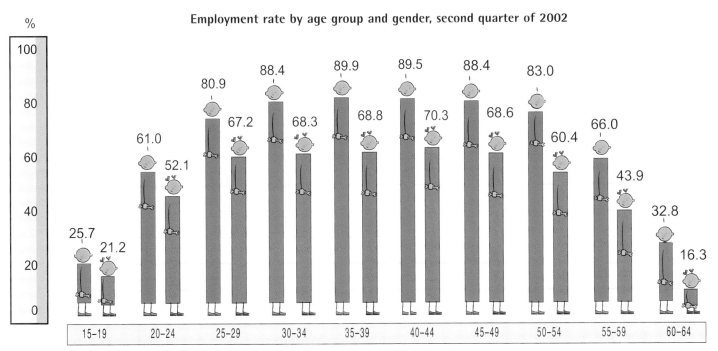

%

	15–19	20–24	25–29	30–34	35–39	40–44	45–49	50–54	55–59	60–64
Men	25.7	61.0	80.9	88.4	89.9	89.5	88.4	83.0	66.0	32.8
Women	21.2	52.1	67.2	68.3	68.8	70.3	68.6	60.4	43.9	16.3

Source: Eurostat

Unemployment rates for both men and women vary from one EU country to another. In March 2003, the unemployment rate for women was lowest in Luxembourg and highest in Spain.

If the EU is to be as competitive as possible and, at the same time, support tomorrow's pensioners, it needs to increase the size of its working population. That means attracting more women into the labour market, and keeping people of both genders working longer. The EU is making a special effort to help people of all ages to find jobs and keep them. That includes policies to encourage part-time work and to remove conflicts between career and private life.

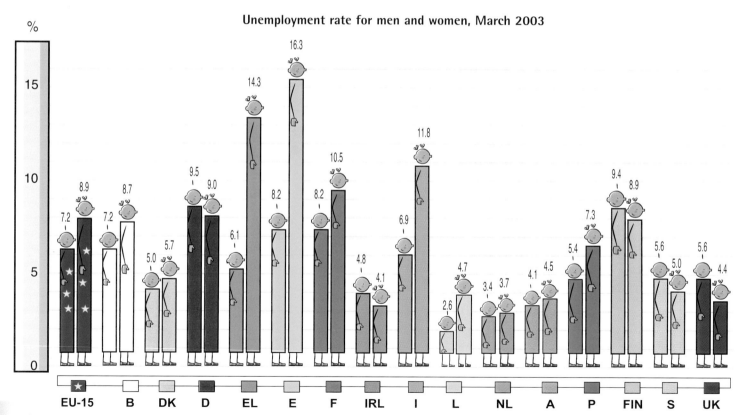

Unemployment rate for men and women, March 2003

%

	EU-15	B	DK	D	EL	E	F	IRL	I	L	NL	A	P	FIN	S	UK
men	7.2	7.2	5.0	9.5	6.1		8.2	4.8	6.9	2.6	3.4	4.1	5.4	9.4	5.6	5.6
women	8.9	8.7	5.7	9.0	14.3	16.3	10.5	4.1	11.8	4.7	3.7	4.5	7.3	8.9	5.0	4.4

Source: Eurostat

Regional differences

Unemployment in the EU affects some regions more than others. It is particularly bad in areas where old industries have shut down, and in outlying regions where not enough has been invested in communications infrastructure. The EU's structural funds (about one third of the EU budget) are used to help regenerate areas of high unemployment, creating new jobs and improving transport links and the environment.

Unemployment rate in EU-15 regions, 2000

Areas where unemployment is 15% or more

Areas where unemployment is between 10% and 15%

Areas where unemployment is between 5% and 10%

Areas where unemployment is less than 5%

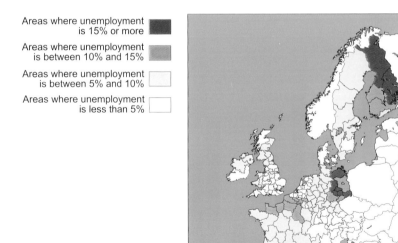

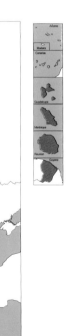

Source: Eurostat

Trade and the economy

One of the EU's main aims is economic progress. Over the last 50 years, and especially since the 1980s, a lot of work has been done to break down the barriers between the EU's national economies and to create a single market where goods, people, money and services can move around freely. Trade between EU countries has greatly increased and at the same time the EU has become a major world trading power.

How much does the EU produce?

Until recently, the GDP of the EU as a whole was similar to that of its main competitor, the United States. In recent years, however, the United States has overtaken the EU - partly thanks to the internet revolution. Europe is now making a special effort to catch up and to take the lead again.

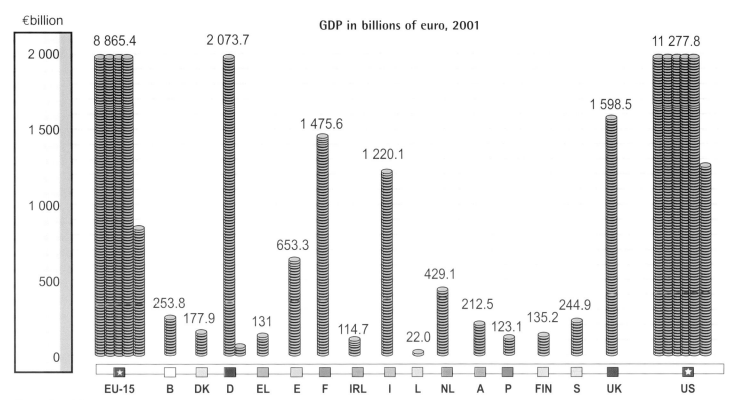

€billion

GDP in billions of euro, 2001

8 865.4	EU-15
253.8	B
177.9	DK
2 073.7	D
131	EL
653.3	E
1 475.6	F
114.7	IRL
1 220.1	I
22.0	L
429.1	NL
212.5	A
123.1	P
135.2	FIN
244.9	S
1 598.5	UK
11 277.8	US

Axis values: 0, 500, 1 000, 1 500, 2 000

Source: Eurostat

GDP in trillions of euro, United States and EU-15, 1991–2001

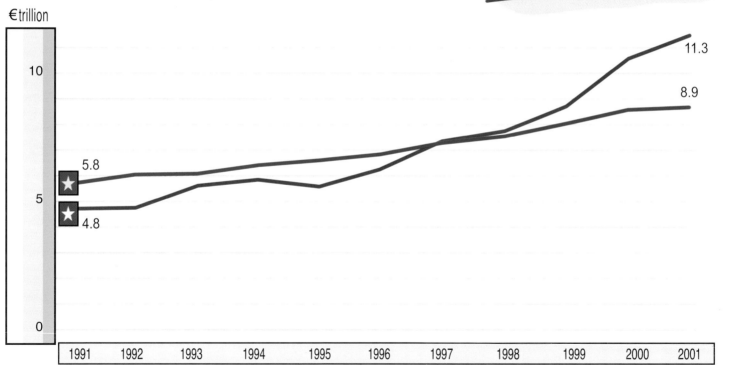

€trillion

10

5.8

5

4.8

0

1991 1992 1993 1994 1995 1996 1997 1998 1999 2000 2001

11.3

8.9

Source: Eurostat

Beating inflation

In the 1980s and early 1990s, one of Europe's major economic problems was inflation – with prices and wages forcing each other upwards. This made it expensive to employ people, and many firms had to lay off workers. To keep inflation in check, central banks had to impose high interest rates that were bad for small businesses and homeowners.

Over the last decade, EU governments have made a concerted effort to bring down inflation and, with it, interest rates and unemployment. Low inflation and low interest rates were among the requirements for countries wishing to adopt Europe's single currency, the euro. The European Central Bank, which sets interest rates throughout the euro zone, aims to keep inflation below 2%.

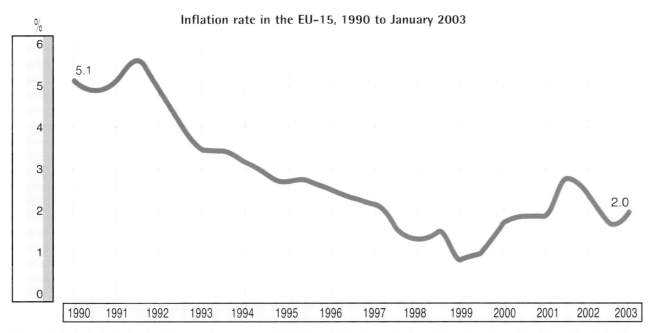

Inflation rate in the EU-15, 1990 to January 2003

The method of calculation for the EU was not harmonised until 1995, so all inflation rates before 1996 are based on national data adopted for the purposes of harmonisation.
Source: Eurostat

The EU: a major trading power

Between 1990 and 2000, the EU's total trade with the rest of the world doubled in value. The European Union is now:

- the world's leading exporter of goods: over €985 billion in 2001, almost a fifth of the world total;
- the world's leading exporter of services: €307 billion in 2001, nearly a quarter of the world total. Services include things like tourism, banking, insurance and transport.

% **The EU's share of the world's total trade in goods, 2001, compared with Japan and the United States**

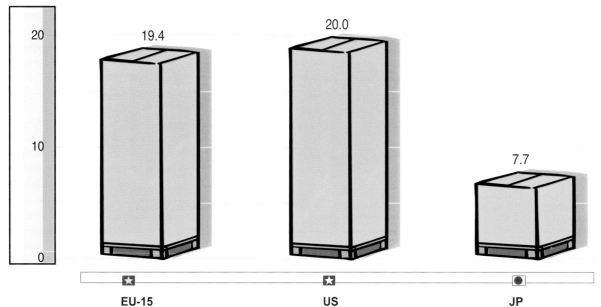

EU-15 — 19.4
US — 20.0
JP — 7.7

Source: Eurostat

The EU's share of the world's total trade in services, 2001, compared with Japan and the United States

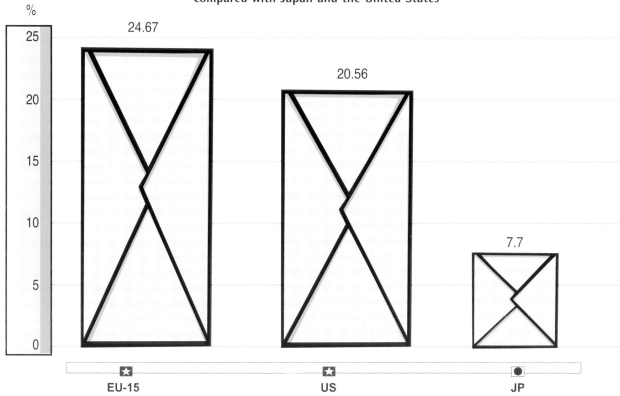

%

24.67

20.56

7.7

EU-15　　　　　US　　　　　JP

Source: Eurostat

The EU's status as a major trading power gives it great responsibility for shaping the future of globalisation. It seeks to use its influence within the World Trade Organisation to ensure fair rules for world trade and to make globalisation benefit all nations, including the poorest.

In 2000, EU-15 imports from developing countries were worth €432 billion – double the figure for 1990. The European Union imports more agricultural products from developing countries than the combined total of the United States, Canada, Australia, New Zealand and Japan. It is the world's biggest importer of goods of all types from the least-developed countries.

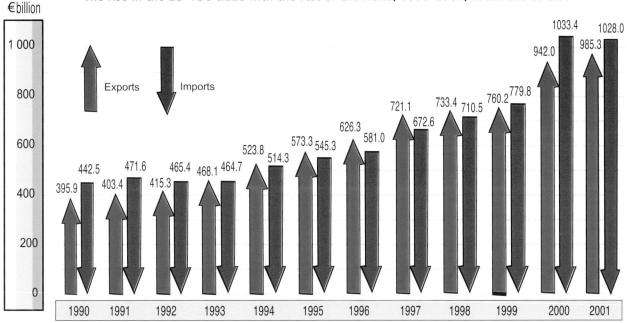

The rise in the EU-15's trade with the rest of the world, 1990-2001, in billions of euro

€billion

Exports   Imports

Year	Exports	Imports
1990	395.9	442.5
1991	403.4	471.6
1992	415.3	465.4
1993	468.1	464.7
1994	523.8	514.3
1995	573.3	545.3
1996	626.3	581.0
1997	721.1	672.6
1998	733.4	710.5
1999	760.2	779.8
2000	942.0	1033.4
2001	985.3	1028.0

Source: Eurostat

Trade between EU countries is also very important, and has become much easier and cheaper thanks to the removal of tariff barriers and customs duties. Intra-EU trade in goods nearly doubled in value between 1990 and 2000. In the case of Ireland it nearly quadrupled.

Exports of goods to other EU countries, as a percentage of total national exports of goods, 2001

%

	EU-15	B	DK	D	EL	E	F	IRL	I	L	NL	A	P	FIN	S	UK
	61.8	74.8	65.7	55.1	41.0	71.4	60.8	63.0	53.8	86.9	78.7	61.5	80.1	53.7	54.6	57.5

Source: Eurostat

Transport, energy and the environment

Transport and energy are vital to the EU economy. Europeans and the products they consume in ever increasing quantity and variety are carried across the continent by all modes of transport – but most of all by road.

As the economy grows, so does the demand for transport and energy. But this growth means increasing congestion and fuel consumption, which in turn create more pollution. These are Europe-wide problems that require Europe-wide solutions decided at EU level.

Going places

Railways and inland waterways (i.e. rivers and canals), once so important for carrying goods and passengers around Europe, now carry only a fifth of the total. Three quarters go by road. The graph shows, in percentage terms, how Europe's total inland transport industry is shared among different modes of transport, and how these shares have changed over recent decades.

Percentage of the total inland transport (in tonne – kilometres), per mode, 1980 and 2000

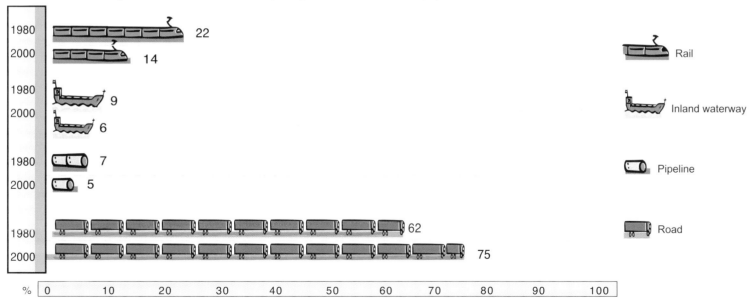

Figures cover the EU-15, Iceland, Liechtenstein, Norway and Switzerland.

Source: Eurostat

Air transport has also increased rapidly over the last two decades, creating congestion at Europe's airports. To tackle this problem, the EU is working towards a unified European system of air traffic control (the 'Single European Sky').

To ease congestion on the roads, the EU is encouraging transport firms to get as much freight as possible onto trains, barges and ships. It is also backing local authorities in their efforts to promote and improve public transport, especially in Europe's crowded cities.

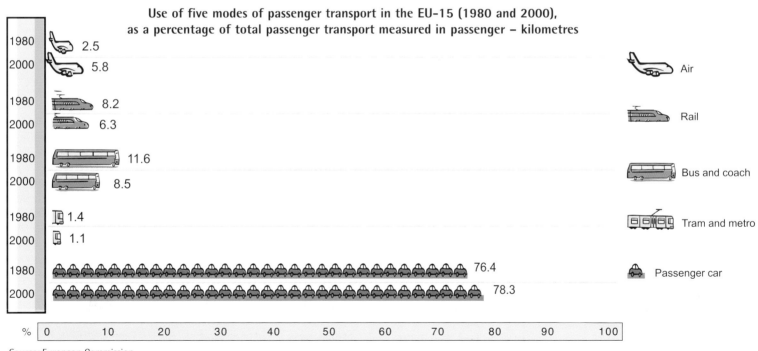

Use of five modes of passenger transport in the EU-15 (1980 and 2000), as a percentage of total passenger transport measured in passenger – kilometres

Year	Air	Rail	Bus and coach	Tram and metro	Passenger car
1980	2.5	8.2	11.6	1.4	76.4
2000	5.8	6.3	8.5	1.1	78.3

Source: European Commission.

Power for the people

'Primary energy' is energy extracted from natural sources – coal, lignite, crude oil, natural gas, nuclear fuel and renewable sources such as wind, water, solar and geothermal energy. The graph shows what percentage of the EU's total production of primary energy is derived from each of these sources.

Production of primary energy in the EU–15, percentage per source, 2001

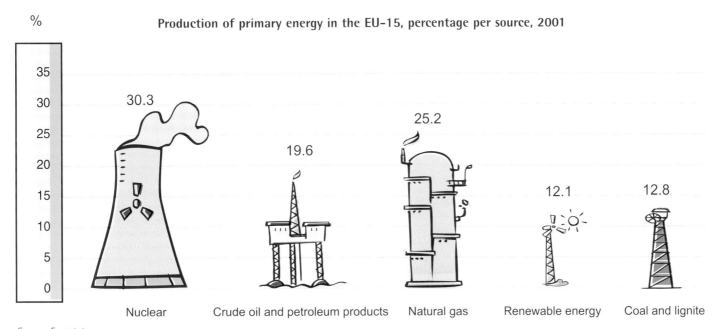

Nuclear	Crude oil and petroleum products	Natural gas	Renewable energy	Coal and lignite
30.3	19.6	25.2	12.1	12.8

Source: Eurostat

Two EU countries (Denmark and the United Kingdom) are net exporters of energy, thanks to their North Sea oil and gas reserves, but the EU as a whole produces only about half the energy it consumes. The rest has to be imported.

Dependence on imported energy, especially on oil, makes Europe vulnerable to international political crises, such as the oil crisis in 1973. So the EU is working hard to develop its own energy resources.

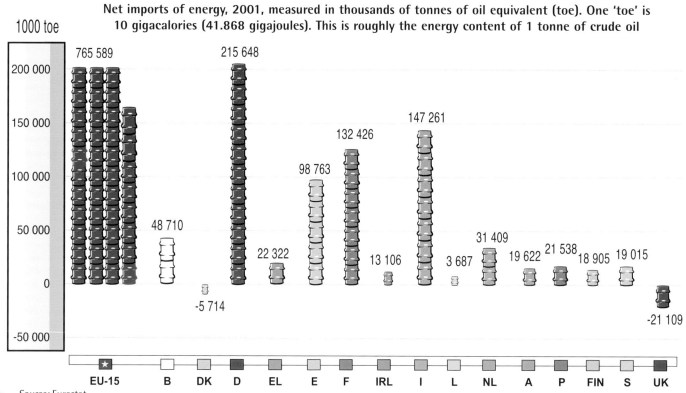

Net imports of energy, 2001, measured in thousands of tonnes of oil equivalent (toe). One 'toe' is 10 gigacalories (41.868 gigajoules). This is roughly the energy content of 1 tonne of crude oil

1000 toe

EU-15	765 589		
D	215 648		
I	147 261		
F	132 426		
E	98 763		
B	48 710		
NL	31 409		
EL	22 322		
P	21 538		
FIN	19 622		
S	19 015		
A	18 905		
IRL	13 106		
L	3 687		
DK	-5 714		
UK	-21 109		

Axis values: 200 000 · 150 000 · 100 000 · 50 000 · 0 · -50 000

EU-15   B   DK   D   EL   E   F   IRL   I   L   NL   A   P   FIN   S   UK

Individually, Europeans consume less energy than US or Japanese citizens. Nevertheless, energy demand in most countries is growing, so we need to develop ever more energy-efficient technologies – such as car engines that consume less petrol.

Consumption of primary energy per person (toe per capita), 1990–2001, in the EU–15, United States and Japan

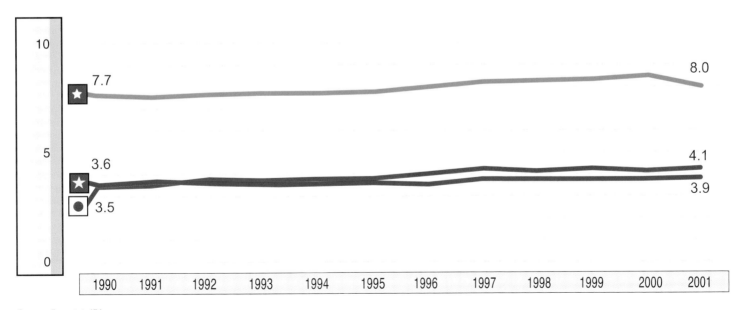

Source: Eurostat, IEA

At one time, the EU generated a large part of its electric power from coal and lignite, which were abundant natural resources. But as reserves have dwindled, coal mining in many countries has become too expensive. Meanwhile, huge reserves of natural gas (a relatively clean fuel) have become available, so power plants have been switching from solid fuels to gas.

However, reserves of all fossil fuels are limited, and burning them releases carbon dioxide (CO_2) into the atmosphere, contributing to global warming. So the EU is putting extra effort into developing clean, renewable energy resources.

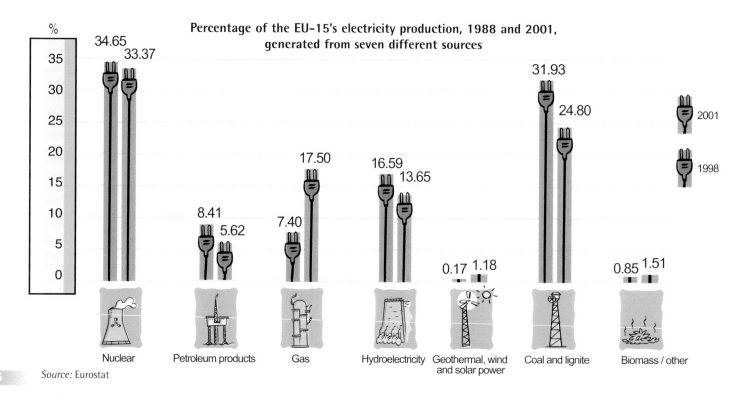

Percentage of the EU-15's electricity production, 1988 and 2001, generated from seven different sources

Source	2001	1998
Nuclear	34.65	33.37
Petroleum products	8.41	5.62
Gas	7.40	17.50
Hydroelectricity	16.59	13.65
Geothermal, wind and solar power	0.17	1.18
Coal and lignite	31.93	24.80
Biomass / other	0.85	1.51

Source: Eurostat

Household gas and electricity prices vary considerably from one EU country to another, especially when national taxes are taken into account. To bring prices down, the EU is opening up national electricity and gas markets to greater competition and, at the same time, developing trans-European networks that will deliver energy more cheaply and efficiently throughout the EU.

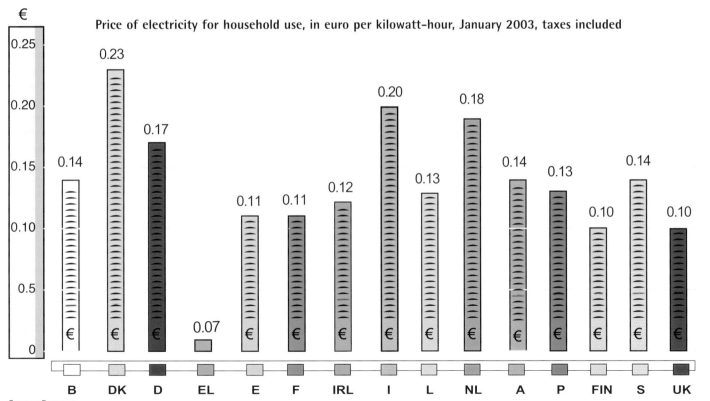

Price of electricity for household use, in euro per kilowatt-hour, January 2003, taxes included

B	DK	D	EL	E	F	IRL	I	L	NL	A	P	FIN	S	UK
0.14	0.23	0.17	0.07	0.11	0.11	0.12	0.20	0.13	0.18	0.14	0.13	0.10	0.14	0.10

Source: Eurostat

Price of natural gas for household use, in euro per gigajoule, January 2003, taxes included

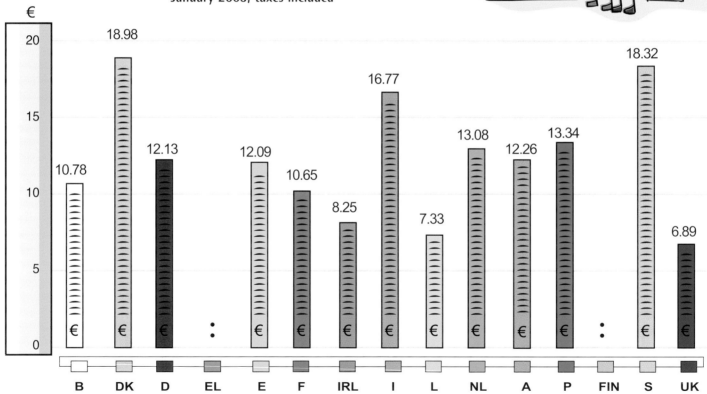

B	DK	D	EL	E	F	IRL	I	L	NL	A	P	FIN	S	UK
10.78	18.98	12.13	:	12.09	10.65	8.25	16.77	7.33	13.08	12.26	13.34	:	18.32	6.89

No figures are available for Finland or Greece, as few households in these countries use natural gas.
Source: Eurostat

Protecting the environment

Pollution recognises no frontiers, so it cannot be tackled effectively by individual countries working in isolation. That is why Europe-wide measures are needed to protect the environment. Sustainable development is a top priority for the EU, which takes environmental concerns into account in all its policy-making.

By burning fossil fuels, Europe puts carbon dioxide (CO_2) into the atmosphere. CO_2 is a 'greenhouse gas' that contributes to the problem of global warming. So the EU is working with its global partners to cut greenhouse gas emissions. By signing the Kyoto Protocol it has committed itself to stabilising these emissions from 2000 onwards. The situation varies from one country to another but, in the EU as a whole, emissions are lower now than in 1990. However, action is needed to help curb the rising emissions from transport.

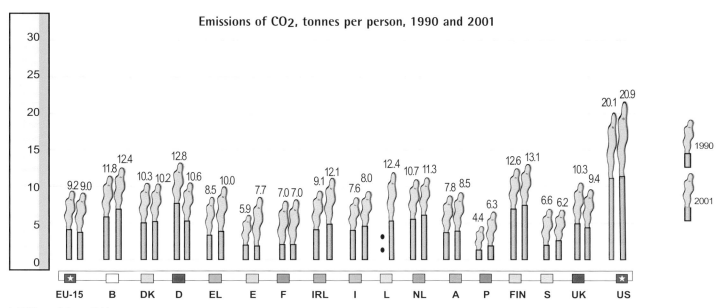

Emissions of CO_2, tonnes per person, 1990 and 2001

EU-15: 9.2 9.0
B: 11.8 12.4
DK: 10.3 10.2
D: 12.8 10.6
EL: 8.5 10.0
E: 5.9 7.7
F: 7.0 7.0
IRL: 9.1 12.1
I: 7.6 8.0
L: 12.4
NL: 10.7 11.3
A: 7.8 8.5
P: 4.4 6.3
FIN: 12.6 13.1
S: 6.6 6.2
UK: 10.3 9.4
US: 20.1 20.9

1990
2001

L 1990: no data available

Sources: UNFCCC, European Environment Agency, Eurostat.

Water pollution is another challenge for the EU. For example, rainwater carries fertilisers from farmland into streams and rivers, damaging the freshwater environment. To tackle this problem, European farmers are cutting back on their use of chemical fertilisers (phosphate, nitrogen and potash).

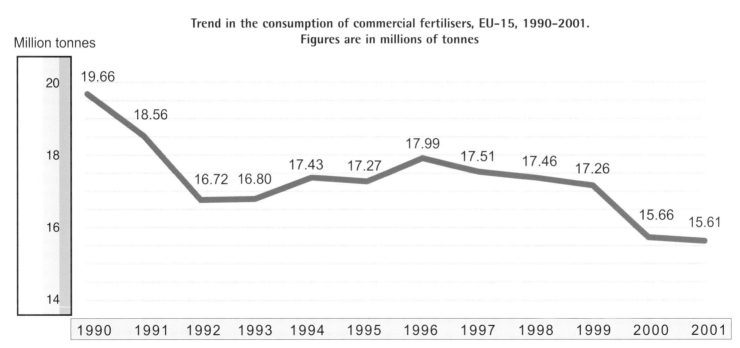

Trend in the consumption of commercial fertilisers, EU-15, 1990–2001.
Figures are in millions of tonnes

Million tonnes

Year	Value
1990	19.66
1991	18.56
1992	16.72
1993	16.80
1994	17.43
1995	17.27
1996	17.99
1997	17.51
1998	17.46
1999	17.26
2000	15.66
2001	15.61

Source: European Commission; United Nations, FAOSTAT

Recycling waste such as used paper and glass is also good for the environment. It saves trees, energy and landfill space and cuts air pollution. Most EU countries have made progress on this front.

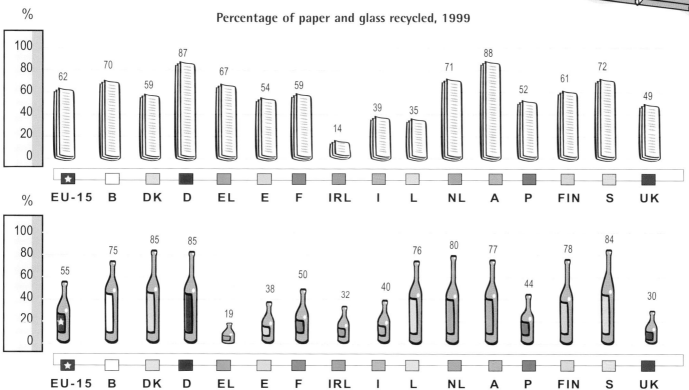

Percentage of paper and glass recycled, 1999

Paper recycling:
EU-15: 62, B: 70, DK: 59, D: 87, EL: 67, E: 54, F: 59, IRL: 14, I: 39, L: 35, NL: 71, A: 88, P: 52, FIN: 61, S: 72, UK: 49

Glass recycling:
EU-15: 55, B: 75, DK: 85, D: 85, EL: 19, E: 38, F: 50, IRL: 32, I: 40, L: 76, NL: 80, A: 77, P: 44, FIN: 78, S: 84, UK: 30

Source: European Commission.

Europeans living together

Increasingly, EU citizens are getting to know one another and developing their sense of belonging together as Europeans. Many spend their holidays in another European country, and increasing numbers of people go to study or work abroad, thanks to freedom of movement within the EU. Also, a high percentage of European school pupils learn at least one European language besides their own.

Chatting with the neighbours

According to a survey in December 2000:

- 53% of Europeans say they can speak at least one European language in addition to their mother tongue;

- 26% of Europeans say they can speak two foreign languages;

- besides their mother tongue, people in Europe tend to know English (41%), French (19%), German (10%), Spanish (7%) and Italian (3%);

- overall, English is the language most often spoken as a first foreign language in Europe.

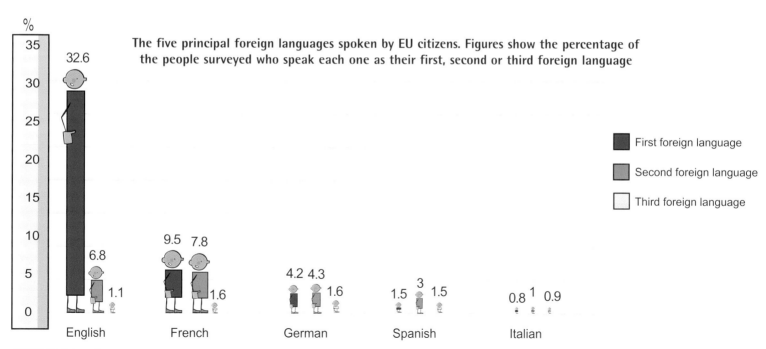

The five principal foreign languages spoken by EU citizens. Figures show the percentage of the people surveyed who speak each one as their first, second or third foreign language

- ■ First foreign language
- ■ Second foreign language
- □ Third foreign language

Source: Eurobarometer.

Working together

The number of EU citizens working in another EU country has risen as more people discover the opportunities available. Freedom of movement has become a reality in the European single market.

Number of EU citizens (men and women separately) working in another EU country, 1997 and 2002

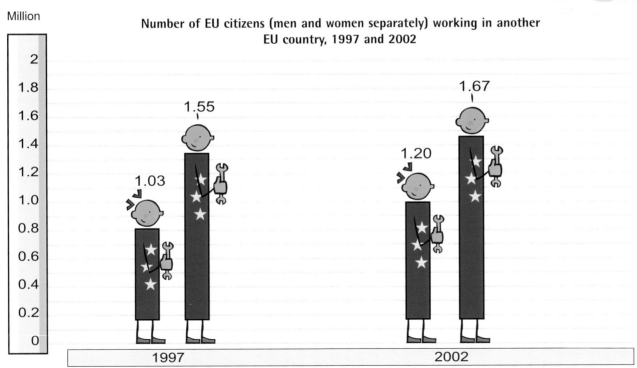

Million

The figures do not include foreigners working in Italy.

Source: EC

Studying together

Increasing numbers of young people are following educational courses in European countries other than their home country. This is largely thanks to EU schemes such as the Erasmus programme which has provided mobility in Europe for more than a million students since it began in 1987.

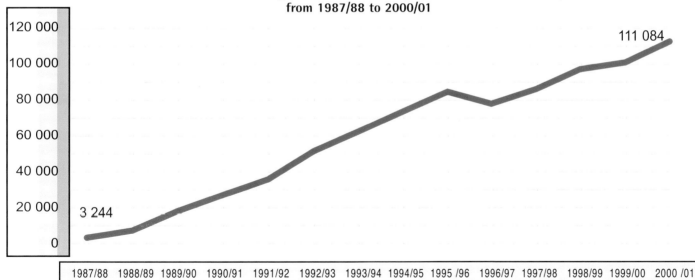

Number of students taking part in the Erasmus programme, each academic year from 1987/88 to 2000/01

111 084

3 244

| 120 000 | 100 000 | 80 000 | 60 000 | 40 000 | 20 000 | 0 |

| 1987/88 | 1988/89 | 1989/90 | 1990/91 | 1991/92 | 1992/93 | 1993/94 | 1994/95 | 1995 /96 | 1996/97 | 1997/98 | 1998/99 | 1999/00 | 2000 /01 |

Source: European Commission.

Feeling European

Public support for the EU varies from country to country and fluctuates over time. According to a Eurobarometer survey (May 2002), approval of EU membership is weakest in prosperous countries that joined the EU relatively recently (Austria, Finland, Sweden) and in the United Kingdom – which has a notably 'Euro-sceptic' press. Support is strongest in Luxembourg (one of the original six member states, with a high standard of living) and in Ireland, which has prospered significantly since joining the EU.

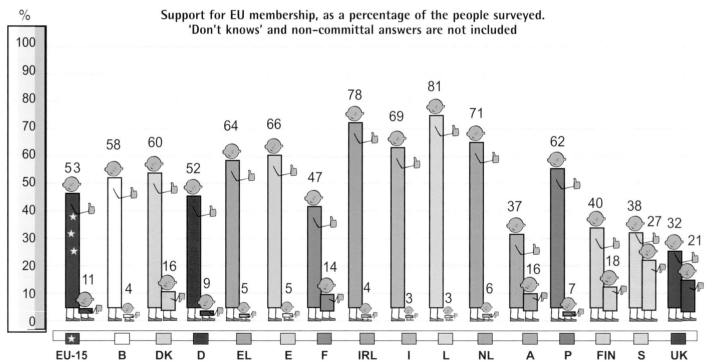

Support for EU membership, as a percentage of the people surveyed.
'Don't knows' and non-committal answers are not included

%

100 90 80 70 60 50 40 30 20 10 0

| EU-15 | B | DK | D | EL | E | F | IRL | I | L | NL | A | P | FIN | S | UK |

EU-15: 53 / 11
B: 58 / 4
DK: 60 / 16
D: 52 / 9
EL: 64 / 5
E: 66 / 5
F: 47 / 14
IRL: 78 / 4
I: 69 / 3
L: 81 / 3
NL: 71 / 6
A: 37 / 16
P: 62 / 7
FIN: 40 / 18
S: 38 / 27
UK: 32 / 21

Source: Eurobarometer.

In Spring 2002, the Eurobarometer survey asked a representative sample of EU citizens the following question: 'Would you say you are very proud, fairly proud, not very proud or not at all proud to be European?'. A quarter of those who responded felt not very or not at all proud to be European. This may be due to lack of public awareness of what the EU is doing or to disappointment with the perceived results. Either way, the EU clearly has to do more to inform its citizens and to give them a greater say in European decision-making. These are now top priorities for European leaders.

Degree of pride in being European, as a percentage of the people surveyed.
'Don't knows' are not included

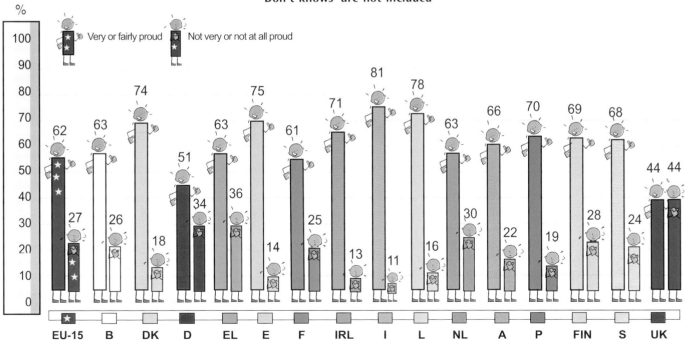

%

Very or fairly proud   Not very or not at all proud

	EU-15	B	DK	D	EL	E	F	IRL	I	L	NL	A	P	FIN	S	UK
Very or fairly proud	62	63	74	51	63	75	61	71	81	78	63	66	70	69	68	44
Not very or not at all proud	27	26	18	34	36	14	25	13	11	16	30	22	19	28	24	44

Source: Eurobarometer.

New member states and candidate countries

The 13 countries covered in this chapter were all given the status of candidates for European Union membership. Before a candidate country can join the EU it must have a stable system of democratic government, and institutions that ensure the rule of law and respect for human rights. It must also have a functioning and competitive market economy.

Ten of the 13 candidates have met all these requirements, completed membership negotiations and are part of the EU from 1 May 2004. Two others (Bulgaria and Romania) expect to follow in 2007. Turkey is the 13th.

How big are they?

Enlargement over the next few years to take in 12 of the 13 candidate countries will increase the EU's population by over 100 million, and its surface area by more than one million square kilometres. With Turkey, the EU would have an extra 70 million people and increase its surface area by more than 18%.

1 000 km²

Surface area, in thousands of square kilometres

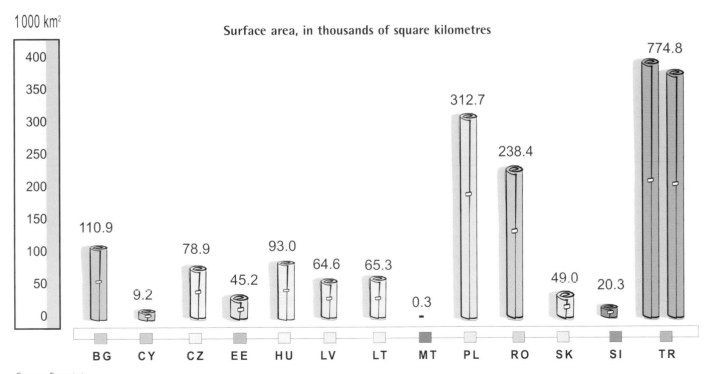

110.9	9.2	78.9	45.2	93.0	64.6	65.3	0.3	312.7	238.4	49.0	20.3	774.8
BG	CY	CZ	EE	HU	LV	LT	MT	PL	RO	SK	SI	TR

Source: Eurostat

♟♟♟ How many people live there?

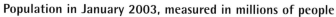

Population in January 2003, measured in millions of people

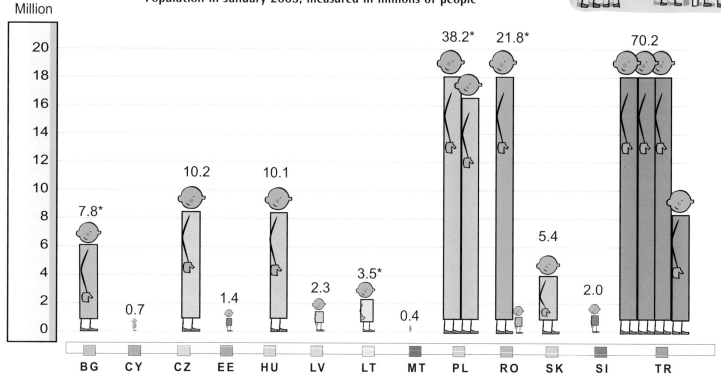

BG	CY	CZ	EE	HU	LV	LT	MT	PL	RO	SK	SI	TR

Source: Eurostat

The population density varies considerably, from crowded Malta to sparsely populated Estonia. In general, the figure is lower than the EU-15 average of 120.2 people per square kilometre.

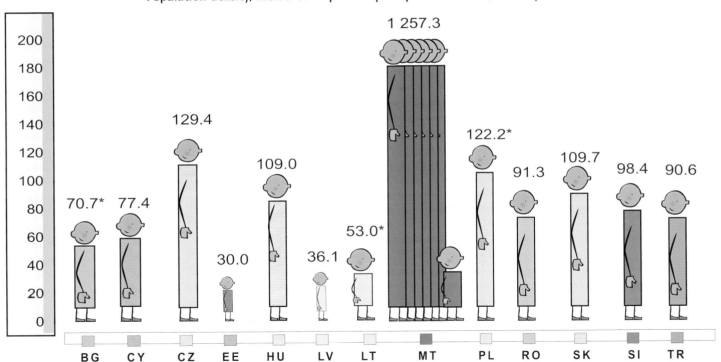

Population density, measured in persons per square kilometre, January 2003

BG	CY	CZ	EE	HU	LV	LT	MT	PL	RO	SK	SI	TR
70.7*	77.4	129.4	30.0	109.0	36.1	53.0*	1 257.3	122.2*	91.3	109.7	98.4	90.6

Source: Eurostat

Making economic progress

The 10 new member states and the three remaining candidate countries are, at present, less wealthy than most other EU countries, and they all have different levels of prosperity. Wealth per inhabitant (GDP per capita) is greatest in small, prosperous countries like Cyprus and Slovenia.

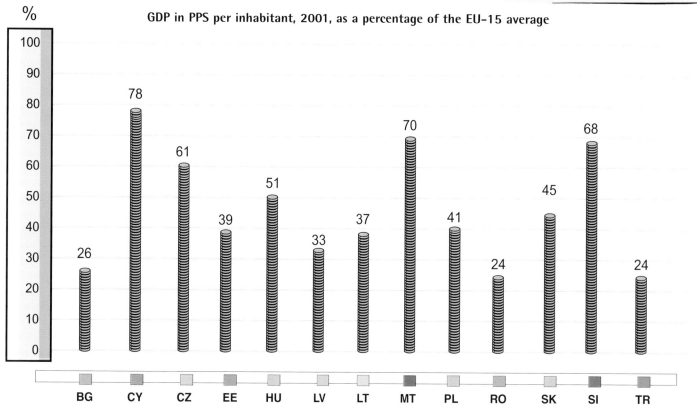

GDP in PPS per inhabitant, 2001, as a percentage of the EU–15 average

%

	BG	CY	CZ	EE	HU	LV	LT	MT	PL	RO	SK	SI	TR
	26	78	61	39	51	33	37	70	41	24	45	68	24

Source: Eurostat

Over the past decade, all the candidate countries have developed thriving market economies. Major economic reforms are creating new jobs and an overall level of economic growth (5% in 2000) that exceeds the EU-15 average.

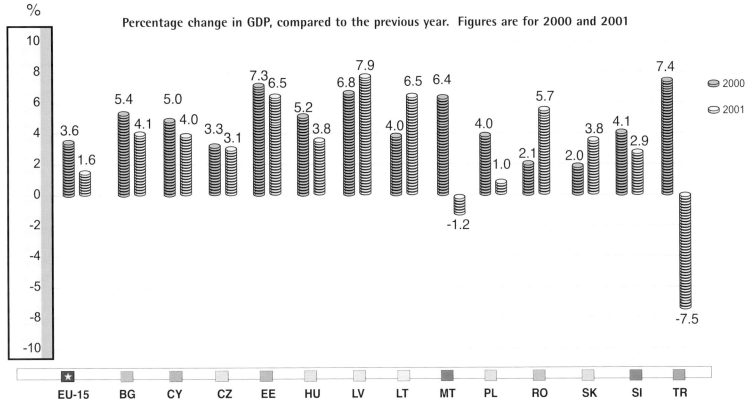

Percentage change in GDP, compared to the previous year. Figures are for 2000 and 2001

%

Legend: ● 2000 ● 2001

	2000	2001
EU-15	3.6	1.6
BG	5.4	4.1
CY	5.0	4.0
CZ	3.3	3.1
EE	7.3	6.5
HU	5.2	3.8
LV	6.8	7.9
LT	4.0	6.5
MT	6.4	-1.2
PL	4.0	1.0
RO	2.1	5.7
SK	2.0	3.8
SI	4.1	2.9
TR	7.4	-7.5

Source: Eurostat

 People at work

Economic reforms in the candidate countries have made business and industry leaner and fitter, but this has also meant job losses in some sectors. As in the EU, young people under 25 are much worse affected by unemployment - except in Cyprus and Malta. EU membership is expected to boost growth and employment.

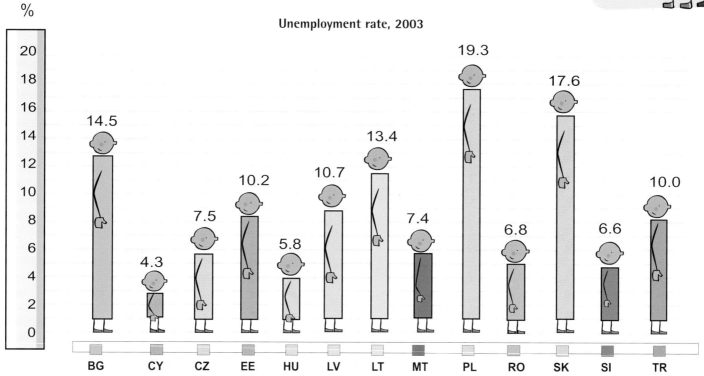

Unemployment rate, 2003

%

BG	CY	CZ	EE	HU	LV	LT	MT	PL	RO	SK	SI	TR
14.5	4.3	7.5	10.2	5.8	10.7	13.4	7.4	19.3	6.8	17.6	6.6	10.0

Source: Eurostat

📁 Education

Citizens of the candidate countries and new member states are, on average, as well educated as other EU citizens. In some countries, the percentage of 18-year-olds still in education is higher than the EU-15 average. In all 13 countries, younger people are better educated than older age groups and higher education greatly reduces the risk of unemployment.

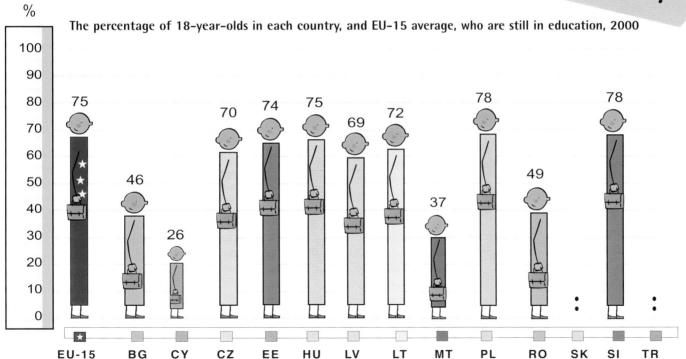

The percentage of 18-year-olds in each country, and EU-15 average, who are still in education, 2000

%

EU-15	BG	CY	CZ	EE	HU	LV	LT	MT	PL	RO	SK	SI	TR
75	46	26	70	74	75	69	72	37	78	49	:	78	:

Figures for Cyprus exclude students studying abroad. Figures for Poland are estimates.

Sources: Unesco, OECD, Eurostat.

The information society: catching up fast

On average, there are fewer personal computers per 100 people in the new member states and candidate countries than in the EU-15, but PC ownership is rising rapidly. Continued economic progress will see the new member states steadily catching up with the rest, and greater use of the internet will, in turn, make their economies more competitive.

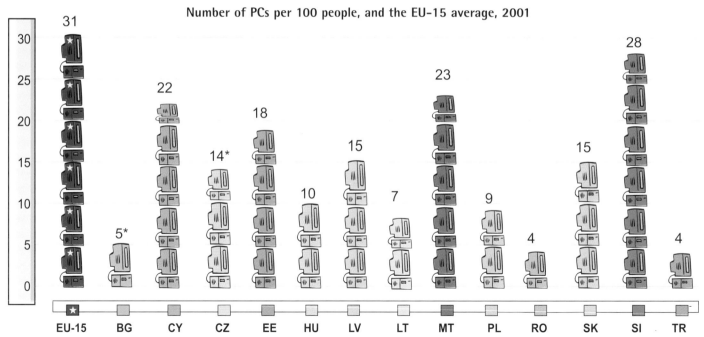

Number of PCs per 100 people, and the EU-15 average, 2001

EU-15	BG	CY	CZ	EE	HU	LV	LT	MT	PL	RO	SK	SI	TR
31	5*	22	14*	18	10	15	7	23	9	4	15	28	4

Source: Eurostat

Since the mid-1990s, mobile phone ownership in the candidate countries and new member states has grown at a spectacular rate.

Number of mobile phone subscribers per 100 people, 2002

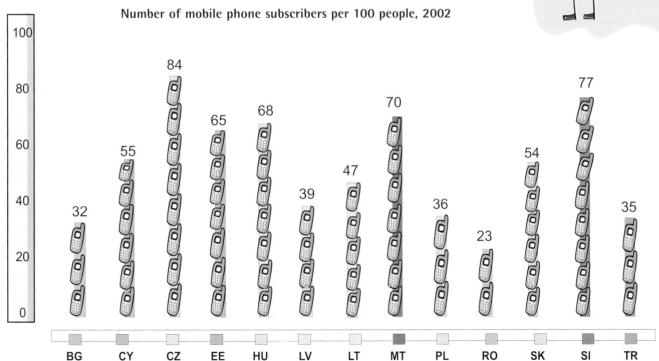

Source: Eurostat

Confident in the future

In May 2003, a Eurobarometer survey asked a representative sample of people in the candidate countries whether EU membership was a good or bad thing. Nearly two thirds (64%) of them said their country would benefit from EU membership. Only 8% said the opposite.

Approval of EU membership, by country, as a percentage of the people surveyed.
'Don't knows' and non-committal answers are not included

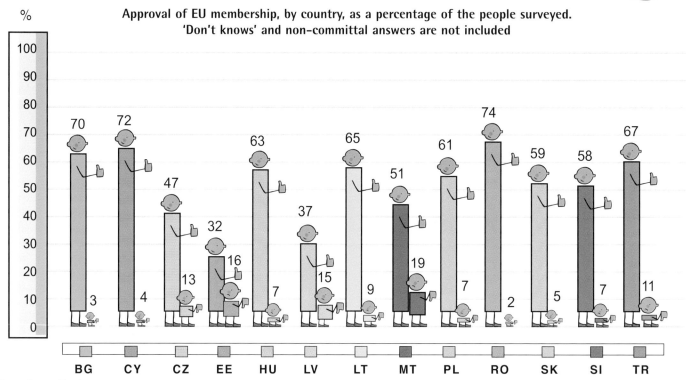

%

	BG	CY	CZ	EE	HU	LV	LT	MT	PL	RO	SK	SI	TR
Approve	70	72	47	32	63	37	65	51	61	74	59	58	67
Oppose	3	4	13	16	7	15	9	19	7	2	5	7	11

Source: Eurobarometer.

Conclusion

With its enlargement in 2004–07, the European Union is grasping a truly historic opportunity – uniting a once-divided continent and creating a peaceful, stable and democratic Europe. This enlargement will also create a single market of nearly half a billion consumers, with excellent potential for economic growth and increasing prosperity.

But peace, democracy, stability and prosperity must not stop at the Union's new borders. That is why the EU will continue forging closer ties with its near neighbours – Russia, Belarus, Ukraine, Moldova, the Caucasus and Balkan regions, the Middle East and North Africa. By working constructively with all these countries on political as well as economic issues, and by giving them easy access to the enlarged single market, the EU aims to spread prosperity, stability and democratic progress throughout its neighbourhood.

Over the period 2000–06, enlargement will cost the EU only about a thousandth of its annual GDP. This is a tiny price to pay for the benefits of a united Europe and a more stable world.

European Commission

**Key facts and figures
about the European Union**

European documentation series

Luxembourg: Office for Official Publications of the European Communities

2004 – 79 pp. – 24.5 x 16.2 cm

ISBN 92-894-6724-X

Summary

The European Union (EU) covers a large part of the continent of Europe. In 2004, its membership increases from 15 to 25. When two more countries join in 2007, the EU will have a population of nearly half a billion.

The European Union aims to be a fair and caring society. All EU countries are committed to peace, democracy, the rule of law and respect for human rights, and they work together to promote these values in the wider world.

To become more competitive and prosperous, the EU is creating new and better jobs and giving its citizens new skills. In partnership with its near neighbours, the EU is also working to spread prosperity and democratic progress beyond its borders.

This booklet sets out many basic facts about the European Union, and presents up-to-date figures in a series of clear and entertaining graphs and illustrations.